I0408121

Copyright © 2017 Moomal M. Soomro

All rights reserved.

In Accordance with the U.S Copyright Act of 1976, the scanning, uploading, and electronic sharing of any part of this book without the permission of the artist/author constitutes unlawful piracy and theft of the artist/author's intellectual property. If you would like to use material from the book (other than for review purposes), prior written permission must be obtained by contacting the artist/author at:

msoomro39@yahoo.com

or visit me on facebook at https://www.facebook.com/momis2

Or follow me at gumroad website at www.gumroad.com/momiart

or follow me on instagram at www.instagram.com/moomal_s

Thank you for your support of the artist/author's rights.
First Printing, 2017

ISBN-13: 978-1546335467

ISBN-10: 1546335463

Aknowledgements

For all the cool colorists across the world who encouraged me to keep on drawing and bringing you yet another book. Thank you so much for your love and encouragement.

And special thanks to my brilliant colorist team who are also motivators for me, Debbie West Cumming, Dee Dee Boseman, Elisabeth Anderson, Jennifer Owen, Jody Ann Savage, Kystal Beasley, Latisha Dollison Lori Delgado, Margolet Van Zyl, Marley Morris, Michelle A. Turner, Tamara Slaten, and Tammy Boykin Lenze.

IMPORTANT INFORMATION FOR USING THIS BOOK

- This book contains 25 hand-drawn illustrations to color, each is printed SINGLE SIDED (back is blank). 25 Fashionable dresses with mannequins!

- The pages are printed on #60 lb bright white paper which performs well for all brands of colored pencils and crayons, without the need of a blotter page.

- To avoid any "Uh Oh's" and the associated disappointment, **Marker and Gel Pen users are STRONGLY ENCOURAGED to USE A BLOTTER SHEET** behind the drawing to avoid any possibility of bleed through to the next page. Several blank blotter and color testing pages are provided at the end of this book.

- Most IMPORTANT of all: Relax, have fun, stand-up and stretch often, and remember that sometimes the most beautiful things come from what we think at first are mistakes, but which turn out to be art's way of working magic!

www.ingramcontent.com/pod-product-compliance
Lightning Source LLC
Chambersburg PA
CBHW081419280526
45788CB00009B/3159